Solos, Duets, and Trios

Favorite Hymn

Book 2

C L A R I N E T

M000106526

FOREWORD

The fifteen pieces in FAVORITE HYMNS can successfully be played as Solos or Duets or Trios, WITH OR WITHOUT piano accompaniment. Any combination of these instruments, Flute, Clarinet, Trumpet and Alto Sax, may be used, although some mixes will be better than others.

Also, the following instruments can participate....

BOOK	ALTERNATE INSTRUMENTS
FLUTE	Piccolo, Violin, Oboe (3rd part)
CLARINET	Tenor Sax (with some 8va.), Bass Clar.
ALTO SAXOPHONE	Alto Clar., Bar. Sax, Mellophone
TRUMPET	Soprano Sax, Baritone TC
PIANO ACCOMPANIMENT	Organ, Synthesizer, Oboe/Recorder (mel.)

FIRST LINE   SOLO PART

SECOND LINE   DUET PART

THIRD LINE   TRIO PART

Rehearsal numbers are indicated in all parts to save rehearsal time.

Duet and Trio parts at times are higher than the Solo part, requiring a downward adjustment in dynamic level so that the melody line is not covered.

In order to enhance musicality and create interest, a considerable amount of contrapuntal writing is included in these arrangements. While the parts are not technically difficult, rhythmic confidence and part independence will be required for satisfactory results.

Project Manager: Carol Cuellar
Cover Illustration: Jorge Paredes
Arranged by Bill Galliford, David Pugh, Ethan Neuberg, and Jackie Worth

WARNER BROS. PUBLICATIONS - THE GLOBAL LEADER IN PRINT
USA: 15800 NW 48th Avenue, Miami, FL 33014

WARNER/CHAPPELL MUSIC
CANADA: 85 SCARSDALE ROAD, SUITE 101
DON MILLS, ONTARIO, M3B 2R2
SCANDINAVIA: P.O. BOX 533, VENDEVAGEN 85 B
S-182 15, DANDERYD, SWEDEN
AUSTRALIA: P.O. BOX 353
3 TALAVERA ROAD, NORTH RYDE N.S.W. 2113

Carisch
NUOVA CARISCH
ITALY: VIA CAMPANIA, 12
20098 S. GIULIANO MILANESE (MI)
ZONA INDUSTRIALE SESTO ULTERIANO
SPAIN: MAGALLANES, 25
28015 MADRID
FRANCE: 25 RUE DE HAUTEVILLE, 75010 PARIS

IMP
INTERNATIONAL MUSIC PUBLICATIONS LIMITED
ENGLAND: SOUTHEND ROAD,
WOODFORD GREEN, ESSEX IG8 8HN
GERMANY: MARSTALLSTR. 8, D-80539 MÜNCHEN
DENMARK: DANMUSIK, VOGNMAGERGADE 7
DK 1120 KOBENHAVNK

Solos, Duets, and Trios

Favorite Hymns

Book 2

C L A R I N E T

CONTENTS

ALL CREATURES OF OUR GOD AND KING

GEISTLICHE KIRCHENGESANGE

Moderately (♩ = 92)

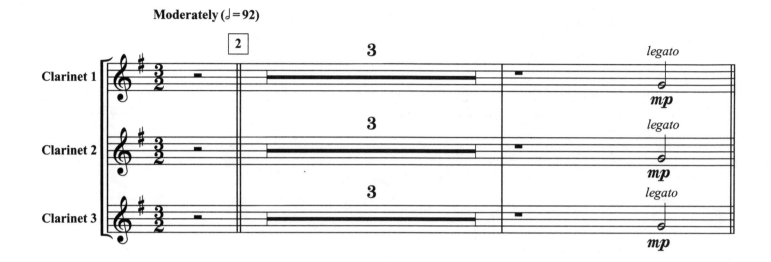

All Creatures of Our God and King - 3 - 1
0127B

4

All Creatures of Our God and King - 3 - 2
0127B

COME, THOU ALMIGHTY KING

TRADITIONAL

Moderately slow (♩ = 80)

Come, Thou Almighty King - 3 - 1
0127B

8

GREAT IS THY FAITHFULNESS

TRADITIONAL

Great Is Thy Faithfulness - 3 - 1
0127B

Great Is Thy Faithfulness - 3 - 3
0127B

HOLY, HOLY, HOLY
LORD GOD ALMIGHTY

Words by
REGINALD HEBER

Music by
JOHN B. DYKES

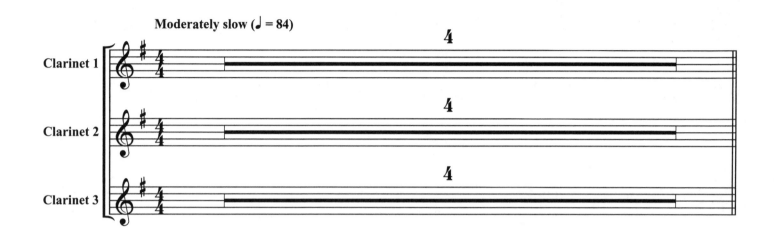

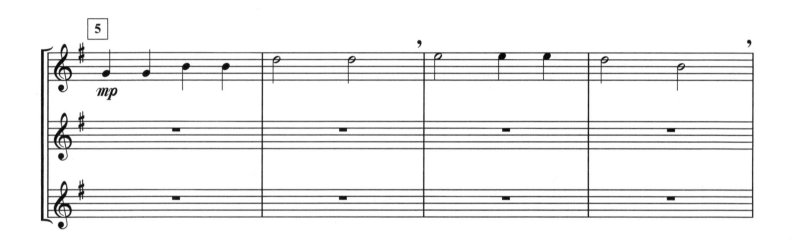

Holy, Holy, Holy - 3 - 1
0127B

Holy, Holy, Holy - 3 - 2
0127B

14

Holy, Holy, Holy - 3 - 3
0127B

I NEED THEE EVERY HOUR

TRADITIONAL

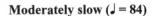

I Need Thee Every Hour - 3 - 1
0127B

16

I Need Thee Every Hour - 3 - 2
0127B

IN THE GARDEN

TRADITIONAL

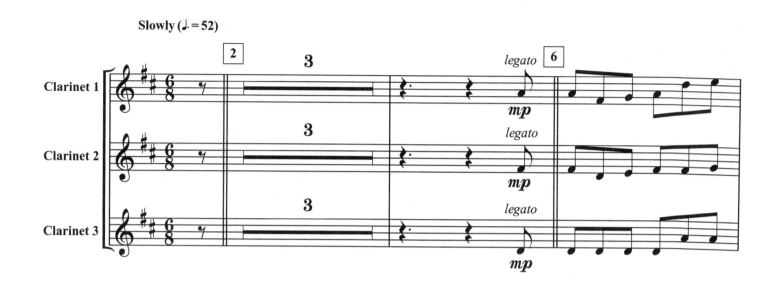

In the Garden - 3 - 1
0127B

In the Garden - 3 - 2
0127B

20

In the Garden - 3 - 3
0127B

LO, HOW A ROSE E'ER BLOOMING

TRADITIONAL

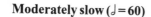

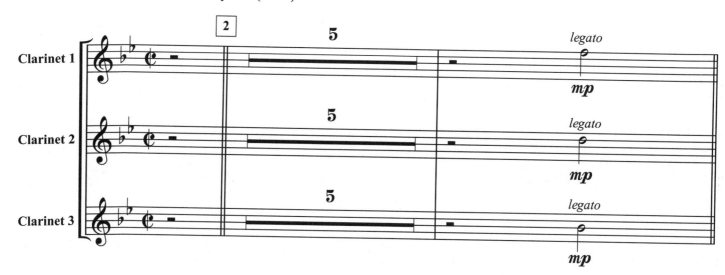

Lo, How a Rose E'er Blooming - 3 - 1
0127B

22

Lo, How a Rose E'er Blooming - 3 - 3
0127B

IT IS WELL WITH MY SOUL

TRADITIONAL

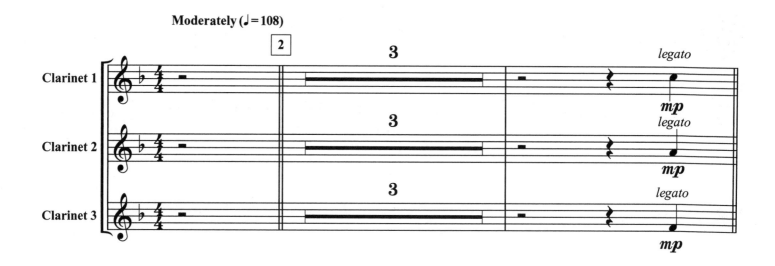

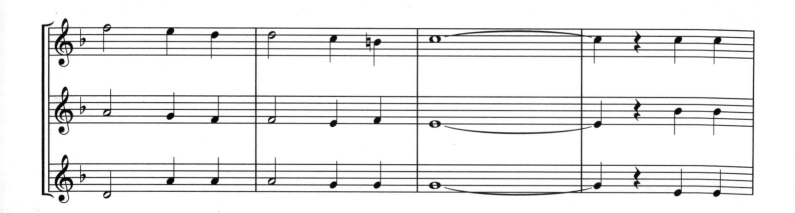

It Is Well With My Soul - 4 - 1
0127B

30

It Is Well With My Soul - 4 - 4
0127B

BE THOU MY VISION

TRADITIONAL IRISH MELODY

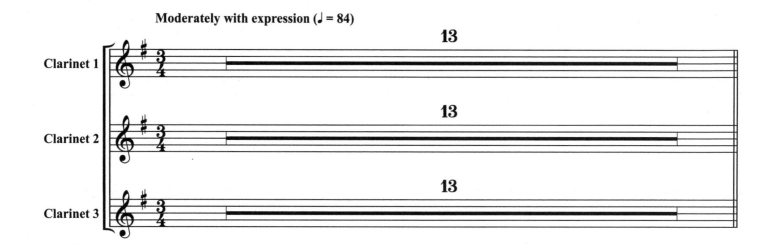

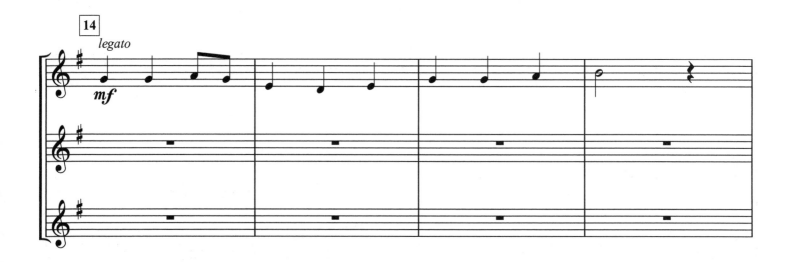

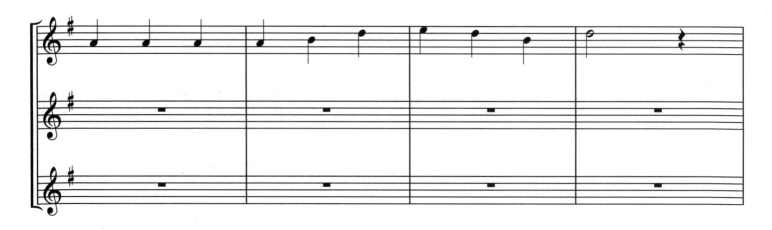

Be Thou My Vision - 3 - 1
0127B

Be Thou My Vision - 3 - 2
0127B

30

Be Thou My Vision - 3 - 3
0127B

INFANT HOLY, INFANT LOWLY

POLISH CAROL

Slowly and gently (♩ = 69)

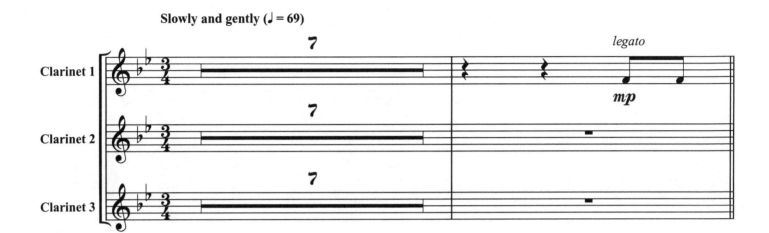

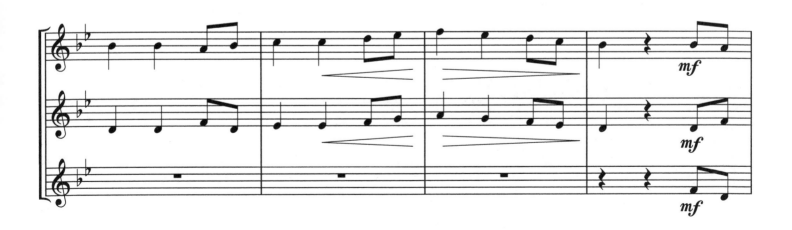

Infant Holy, Infant Lowly - 3 - 1
0127B

Infant Holy, Infant Lowly - 3 - 2
0127B

Infant Holy, Infant Lowly - 3 - 3
0127B

COME THOU FOUNT OF EVERY BLESSING

TRADITIONAL

Moderately slow (♩ = 84)

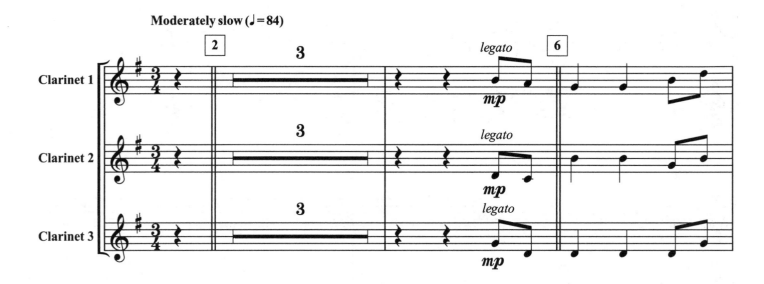

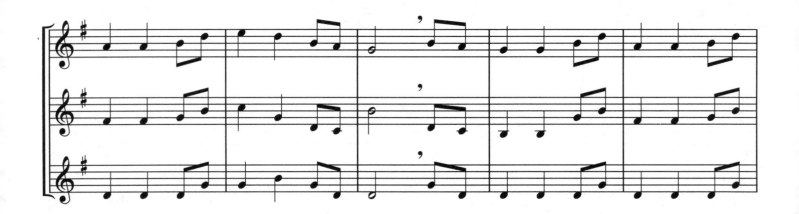

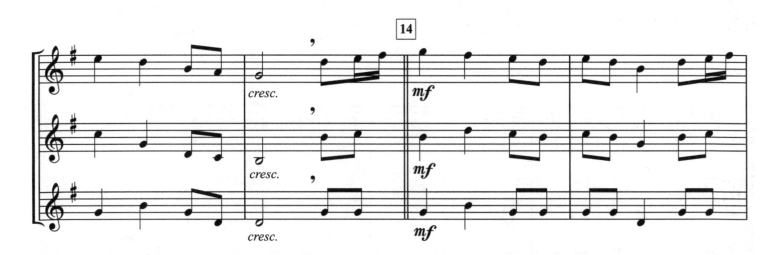

Come, Thou Fount of Every Blessing - 2 - 1
0127B

I LOVE TO TELL THE STORY

Words and Music by
KATHERINE HANKEY
and W. G. FISCHER

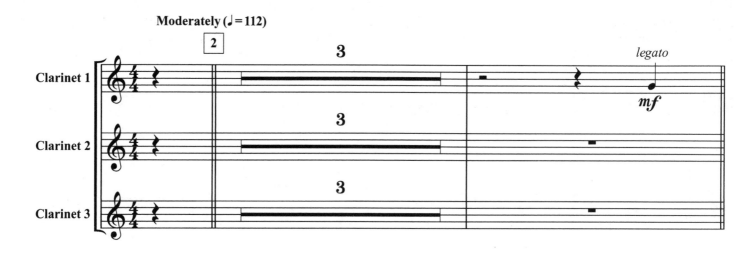

(Play 2nd time only)

(Play 2nd time only)

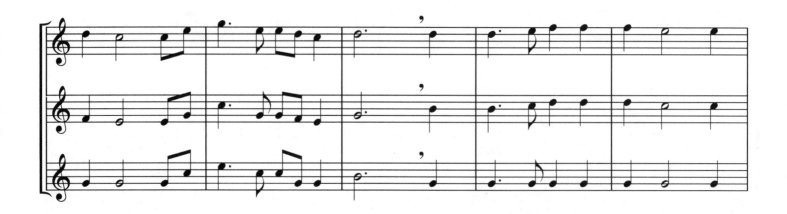

I Love To Tell the Story - 2 - 1
0127B

I Love To Tell the Story - 2 - 2
0127B

COME, THOU LONG-EXPECTED JESUS

TRADITIONAL

Come, Thou Long-Expected Jesus - 4 - 1
0127B

Come, Thou Long-Expected Jesus - 4 - 2
0127B

Come, Thou Long-Expected Jesus - 4 - 4
0127B

O FOR A THOUSAND TONGUES TO SING

TRADITIONAL

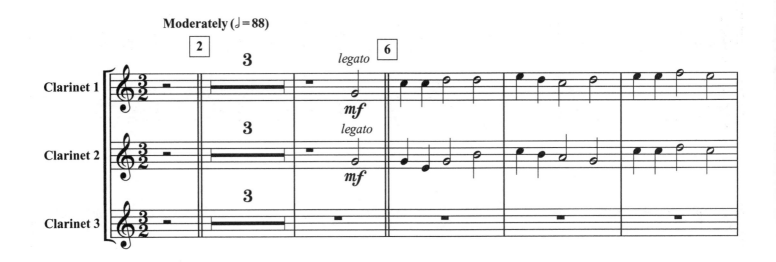

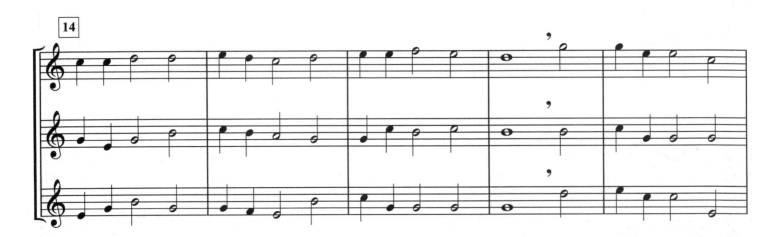

O For a Thousand Tongues To Sing - 2 - 1
0127B

FOR THE BEAUTY OF THE EARTH

Words by
FOLLIOT S. PIERPOINT

Music by
CONRAD KOCHER

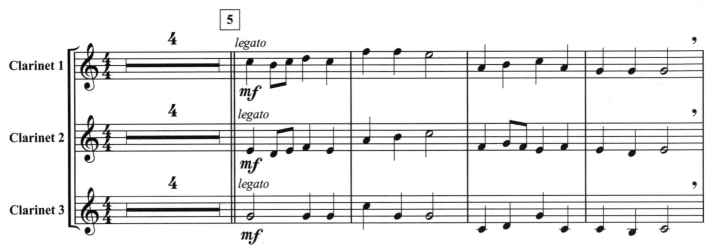

For the Beauty of the Earth - 2 - 1
0127B

For the Beauty of the Earth - 2 - 2
0127B

The Instrumental Favorites Series
(Solos, Duets and Trios with Piano Accompaniment*)

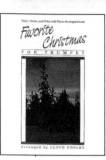

Favorite Christmas, Volume 2
arranged by Lloyd Conley
(F3260FLX) Flute
(F3260CLX) Clarinet
(F3260ASX) Alto Sax
(F3260TSX) Tenor Sax
(F3260TRX) Trumpet
(F3260TBX) Trombone
(F3260PAX) Piano Acc.

Ten Christmas favorites. Titles include: Gesu Bambino (The Infant Jesus) • I'll Be Home for Christmas • It's the Most Wonderful Time of the Year • O Come, All Ye Faithful • Rockin' Around the Christmas Tree • Santa Claus Is Comin' to Town.

Favorite Country Ballads
(IF9554) Flute
(IF9555) Clarinet
(IF9557) Alto Sax
(IF9556) Trumpet
(MF9563) Piano Acc.

Fifteen country greats including: Angels Among Us • The Dance • I Can Love You Like That • I Swear • I Will Always Love You • If I Were You • If Tomorrow Never Comes • In This Life • The Keeper of the Stars • The River • Thinkin' About You • The Wind Beneath My Wings • Your Love Amazes Me.

Favorite Gershwin® Classics
(IF9632) Flute
(IF9633) Clarinet
(IF9634) Alto Sax
(IF9635) Trumpet
(IF9636) Trombone
(IF9637) Piano Acc.

Fourteen Gershwin® classics. Titles include: Let's Call the Whole Thing Off • Embraceable You • 'S Wonderful • I Got Rhythm • Love Walked In • Fascinating Rhythm • I've Got a Crush on You and more.

Favorite Hymns
arranged by Keith Snell
(F2814FLX) Flute
(F2814CLX) Clarinet
(F2814ASX) Alto Sax
(F2814TRX) Trumpet
(F2814PAX) Piano Acc.

A dozen titles, including: Battle Hymn of the Republic • Amazing Grace • Joy to the World • Let Us Break Bread Together • Morning Has Broken • Were You There.

Favorite Jazz Classics
(IF9627) Flute
(IF9628) Clarinet
(IF9629) Alto Sax
(IF9630) Trumpet
(IF9631) Trombone
(IF9626) Piano Acc.

The titles are: The Birth of the Blues • Dreamsville • Elmer's Tune • G.I. Jive • Have You Met Miss Jones? • Lazy River • Love Me, or Leave Me • Straighten Up and Fly Right • The Swinging Shepherd Blues • Taking a Chance on Love • Witchcraft.

Favorite Jazz
arranged by Keith Snell
(F2989FLX) Flute
(F2989CLX) Clarinet
(F2989ASX) Alto Sax
(F2989TRX) Trumpet
(F2989PAX) Piano Acc.

Eight jazz standards. Titles include: Ain't Misbehavin' • Don't Get Around Much Anymore • Five Foot Two, Eyes of Blue • Misty • Satin Doll • Star Dust.

Favorite Latin Standards
arranged by Keith Snell
(F3199CLX) Clarinet
(F3199ASX) Alto Sax
(F3199TRX) Trumpet
(F3199V1X) Violin
(F3199PAX) Piano Acc.

A collection of 15 lively Latin titles arranged at an intermediate level. Includes: Adios • Bésame Mucho • Brazil • Cuando Calienta el Sol • Granada • Guantanamera • Lisbon Antigua • Perfidia • Tico Tico • Vereda Tropical.

Favorite Movie Standards
arranged by Keith Snell
(F3198CLX) Clarinet
(F3198TRX) Trumpet

A collection of 15 great movie titles arranged at an intermediate level. Includes: Chattanooga Choo Choo • Don't Sit Under the Apple Tree • Laura • Mona Lisa • Moon River • Never on Sunday • Over the Rainbow • Singin' in the Rain.

Favorite Wedding Classics
arranged by Keith Snell
(F3228FLX) Flute
(F3228CLX) Clarinet
(F3228ASX) Alto Sax
(F3228TRX) Trumpet
(F3228PAX) Piano Acc.

15 intermediate to advanced level arrangements of the most often requested classical pieces for weddings. Includes "Air" (from *Water Music* - Handel) • Ave Maria (Gounod/J.S. Bach) • Bridal Chorus (from *Lohengrin* - Wagner).

Piano accompaniment is not available for all titles.

THE BEST INSTRUMENTAL BOOKS

We've collected the most popular music from stage, screen, and the top of the charts, and created arrangements for all major instruments. These books have been specifically arranged to work in conjunction with one another, so budding musicians can perform with their friends.

The Best in Popular Sheet Music

(IF9548) Flute
(IF9549) Clarinet
(IF9551) Alto Sax
(IF9552) Tenor Sax
(IF9550) Trumpet
(IF9553) Trombone

Selections include: Angels Among Us • Desperado • From a Distance • Have You Ever Really Loved a Woman? • I Swear • I Will Always Love You • Lane's Theme • Love Will Keep Us Alive • More Than Words • Now and Forever • Over the Rainbow • The Rose • Stairway to Heaven • Tears in Heaven • You Got It and more.

Butterfly Kisses and Other Hot Pop Singles for 1997

(IF9713) Flute
(IF9714) Clarinet
(IF9715) Alto Sax
(IF9716) Tenor Sax
(IF9717) Trumpet
(IF9718) Trombone

Titles are: Because You Loved Me • Butterfly Kisses • By Heart • For You I Will • Gotham City (from *Batman & Robin*) • How Do I Live • I Believe I Can Fly (from *Space Jam*) • MMMBop • Quit Playing Games (With My Heart) • Say You'll Be There • Sunny Came Home • Un-Break My Heart • Until I Find You Again • You Were Meant for Me.

Selections from *Fiddler on the Roof*

(IF9520) Flute
(IF9521) Clarinet
(IF9522) Trumpet
(IF9523) Alto Sax
(IF9524) Tenor Sax
(IF9525) Trombone
(IF9801) Violin
(MF9535) Piano Acc.

All the books are compatible for unison playing in any configuration of instruments and are written specifically to keep each instrument within a comfortable range while maintaining the melodic integrity of the song. The titles are: Anatevka • Do You Love Me? • Far from the Home I Love • Fiddler on the Roof • If I Were a Rich Man • Matchmaker • Miracle of Miracles • Now I Have Everything • Sabbath Prayer • Sunrise, Sunset • To Life • Tradition.

Music from *Batman* 15 Great Themes

(0075B) Flute
(0076B) Clarinet
(0078B) Alto Sax
(0079B) Tenor Sax
(0077B) Trumpet
(0080B) Trombone
(0081B) Piano Acc.

Contains music from all four blockbuster Batman films and the popular TV series. Titles include: The Batman Theme (Elfman) • Batman Theme (TV Version) • Flowers • Poison Ivy • Foolish Games • The Bat Cave • Descent into Mystery • The Lair • Selena Transforms • Rooftop Seduction • Face to Face and more.

Popular Songs of Inspiration

(IF9639) Flute
(IF9640) Clarinet
(IF9641) Alto Sax
(IF9642) Tenor Sax
(IF9643) Trumpet
(IF9644) Trombone
(IF9638) Piano Acc.

This beautiful folio captures all the best of spiritual music with compatible instrumental arrangements of 15 well-known hymns and popular inspirational songs. Titles include: From a Distance • Man in the Mirror • Over the Rainbow • Reach • The River • We Are the World • The Wind Beneath My Wings.

AD298 0398

From the Baroque to the 20th Century

CLASSICAL INSTRUMENTAL ENSEMBLES FOR ALL

CLASSICAL DUETS FOR ALL • CLASSICAL TRIOS FOR ALL
CLASSICAL QUARTETS FOR ALL
Arranged by William Ryden

Any combination and any number of instruments can play together in harmony. Woodwinds, brass, strings and percussion can have fun playing in like instrument or mixed instrument ensembles.

These collections of keyboard, vocal and instrumental pieces cover a wide range of styles and music by composers from the Baroque to the 20th Century periods.

All the music is carefully graded from Level I to Level IV. Alternate musical passages and octaves are provided for some of the selections to allow the player more choices when needed.

The pages are laid out in an identical manner in each book so that all performers can quickly locate a point for discussion or rehearsal. No page turns are required when playing.

This set of books will meet the needs of classmates, friends, family and neighbors who want to play together in school, in church or at the mall. This is also an outstanding tool for auditions, sight reading and learning the art of ensemble playing. These are all-purpose folios that make classical music fun!

CLASSICAL DUETS FOR ALL • CLASSICAL TRIOS FOR ALL • CLASSICAL QUARTETS FOR ALL
fit your every need!

CLASSICAL DUETS FOR ALL
(17 titles)
(EL96127) Piano/Conductor, Oboe
(EL96128) Flute, Piccolo
(EL96129) B♭ Clarinet, Bass Clarinet
(EL96130) Alto Saxophone
      (E♭ Saxes and E♭ Clarinets)
(EL96131) Tenor Saxophone
(EL96132) B♭ Trumpet, Baritone T.C.
(EL96133) Horn in F
(EL96134) Trombone, Baritone B.C.,
      Bassoon, Tuba
(EL96135) Violin
(EL96136) Viola
(EL96137) Cello/Bass
(EL96138) Percussion

CLASSICAL TRIOS FOR ALL
(15 titles)
(EL96139) Piano/Conductor, Oboe
(EL96140) Flute, Piccolo
(EL96141) B♭ Clarinet, Bass Clarinet
(EL96142) Alto Saxophone
      (E♭ Saxes and E♭ Clarinets)
(EL96143) Tenor Saxophone
(EL96144) B♭ Trumpet, Baritone T.C.
(EL96145) Horn in F
(EL96146) Trombone, Baritone B.C.,
      Bassoon, Tuba
(EL96147) Violin
(EL96148) Viola
(EL96149) Cello/Bass
(EL96150) Percussion

CLASSICAL QUARTETS FOR ALL
(13 titles)
(EL96151) Piano/Conductor, Oboe
(EL96152) Flute, Piccolo
(EL96153) B♭ Clarinet, Bass Clarinet
(EL96154) Alto Saxophone
      (E♭ Saxes and E♭ Clarinets)
(EL96155) Tenor Saxophone
(EL96156) B♭ Trumpet, Baritone T.C.
(EL96157) Horn in F
(EL96158) Trombone, Baritone B.C.,
      Bassoon, Tuba
(EL96159) Violin
(EL96160) Viola
(EL96161) Cello/Bass
(EL96162) Percussion